Objective Lessons
Self-Care for Museum Workers

Objective Lessons
Self-Care for Museum Workers

Seema Rao

First Edition: 2017

Library of Congress Cataloging-in-Publication Data
Rao, Seema
Objective Lessons: Self-Care for Museum Workers / Seema Rao-1st ED
p.cm.
ISBN 978-1979203210
1. Self-Help, Creativity 2. Experimental Learning

ISBN-13: 978-1979203210 ISBN-10: 1979203210

14 13 12 11 10 / 10 9 8 7 6 5 4 3 2 1

Contents

"The beginning of the end can feel a lot like the middle
when you are living in it"

-Karen Russell

"Because when you are imagining, you might as well
imagine something worthwhile."

-Lucy Maud Montgomery

Begin

Hello. Welcome. This book is for anyone who works in a museum, aquarium, zoo, historic home...well, basically, any institution that has a collection. Why such a specific audience? Well, we have some distinct cultural norms.

When you work at a place with a collection, the work culture can be *stressful, competitive, disheartening, disappointing, disorganized, unfair, unequal, angering, frustrating, illogical, exhausting*

But, you do it, because *of love, responsibility, respect, honor, care, diligence, trust, passion, personal fulfilment, rewarding, leaves a legacy*

And, so here we are. We have come to this field, and we love it, but there is baggage. So, this is where this book comes in. The goal of this book is to gain some critical distance so that you can act more objectively.

This book is yours, and yours alone. Keep it private. Be honest with yourself. Be kind to yourself. And, most importantly, enjoy.

Helpful Hints

Keep this book private.

Use this book regularly.

Feel free to make mistakes.

Use a pencil, pen, marker, or anything that writes. Avoid erasers. Mistakes are just the path to better lines. //yes!

The book asks you to imagine outlandish outcomes. Go with it.

Try and try again.

Start with You

Just to get you warmed up, take stock. Answer these questions. Don't think too hard. Answer in words and pictures.

What are your three biggest dreams?

Travel
Stable
Save

Who are you?

I am kind and generous. I am a hard worker who likes to nap.

What makes you tick?

Possibilities. Adventure. I like to do/try new things.

What makes you freeze?

Criticism, unfairness, cruelty

What exhausts you?

Arguements; Social interaction; conferences; meetings;

What ignites you? *A goal with a clear path to success. Rewards. Order.*

What is your greatest sadness?
Failure. Regret.

What brings you unspeakable joy?
A job well done; being loved; being respected;

What makes you slow down?
Confusion. Mess. Disorganization. Unclear outcomes.

What is your greatest desire?
To have a job where I make a difference and have authority in reality - not on paper. To lead a team.

About Basic Self-Care

Self-care is one of those phrases that gets overused. But, think of the idea underlying the phrase—the need to keep yourself well.

This book will take you through a series of structured, creative activities. You should do the practices in the book in tandem with activities that keep your mind and body healthy.

Here are a few for you to try. Research more options. Try one body and one mind practice every day for a week. For each, write notes on your feelings. Rate each as a self-care tool for you.

Body	*Notes*
Dance	
Stretch	
Walk/ Run	
Drink Water	
Eat more Vegetables	
Sleep at least 7 hours	— I do this already! Sleep is a priority for me. NAPS.

Mind

Notes

Take ten deep breaths

Write yourself kind notes

Read for pleasure

Call a friend

Visit an outdoor space

Listen to a new musical genre.

Museums

Museums are spaces for people and things. Now, as a museum professional, you will likely have a more nuanced description. But, for this book, let's stick with that definition. In museum life, we often spend an inordinate amount of time on things, however precious, and less time on spaces and people. Most museum people have a finely-honed understanding of "things" from art to dinosaurs, and everything in between.

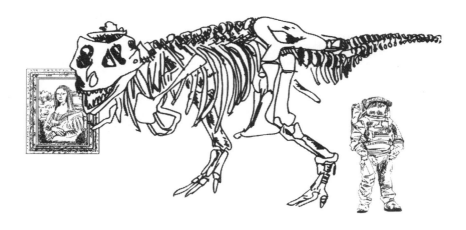

Let's use that strength as a starting point. This book is a collection of exercises that combine object-centered thinking and imagination. I used this contrivance to help you situate yourself in the project, like making sure you are on solid ground before climbing higher up a cliff. But, in the end, each exercise is about people, most of all you.

This book invites you to use imagination as a growth tool. Broadly, you start with a few introductory exercises before getting into the book.

The central section of the book is broken into two parts:

- You: think about yourself,
- You & Work: understanding your ideas about yourself in your career.

Take the book slowly, and in order, like you are going through a special exhibition. Each section is contingent on the previous one. Don't zoom through the book. Go slow. After you finish an exercise, give yourself some time to daydream rather than moving directly on to the next one.

Imagine

Imagination is like wonder crossed with storytelling. But, that description doesn't encompass the feeling of using your imagination. Really, imagination is the feeling of letting your mind travel as far as it chooses. You leave aside mental roadblocks like rationality or doubt. You gain freedom and surprise.

Children are geniuses in their imaginative play. Don't believe me? Ask a 4-year-old to tell you a story about clouds. You will likely be treated to an extraordinary tale.

Learning reasoning, organization, and time-management skills are essential stops on the path to adulthood. Many people concurrently shed their imagination skills. But, imagination is like riding a bike. You did it once, and you can do it again.

Fostering Imagination:
- Give yourself more free time.
- Put away your phone so that you can spend time without diversion.
- Spend time focusing on your senses. Listen, smell, touch.
- Explore your regular life looking for new surprises.
- Look for prompts all around you. Imagine what might be behind that door you pass every day, for example.
- Don't correct yourself when you daydream.
- Don't feel like you need to put your imagined ideas into text. Let them be visual if that is how they appear in your mind.

Gearing Up

Gears are a pretty ingenious in their simplicity. Gears fit together with teeth so that when one spins, the attached wheel turns as well. Gears rotate together to transfer and increase power.

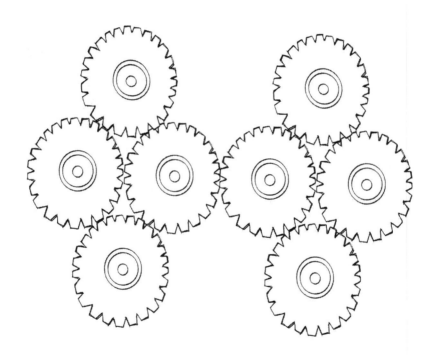

This mechanism summarizes your process through the book. You begin by exposing your negativity. For some of us, this section will be challenging. I would invite you to work through it. But, if you feel genuinely uncomfortable, pick out just a few exercises. Then, you focus on positive feelings. You will want to spend a great deal of time in this section. The subsequent part about imagination need positivity as fuel. Finally, this process ends with planning. This process allows you to take your good feelings and move them into the place where they can become manifest in your life.

You will notice that despite a four-part process, there are eight gears on the facing page. The book is split into two sections: You as well as You & Work. In each section, you will go through this four-part process. The goal is that you are solid about yourself before tackling your feelings about work.

See-Saw

See-Saws are fun, until the weight shifts. Suddenly, the predictable up and down rhythm is broken. The heavy end falls with its inhabitant toppling off head first or the person at the light end stranded mid-air.

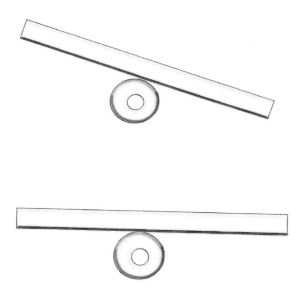

Scholars have mixed feelings on the value of negativity. I won't weigh in on that here. Instead, I invite you to try to think about balance. For some people, their personality is the half-empty kind, neither a weakness nor a fault. Other people wake up singing.

Your goal should be to try to get your negativity into a balance that feels good to you. Your balance will be different than someone else's. Be willing to release your negativity, but be okay with being somewhat cynical.

Start this process by estimating how your seesaw of positivity and negativity looks. If you are pretty close to your best state, then your seesaw will be near balance. If you are overly cynical, the right side will be tipped down. If you are falsely optimistic, the left falls.

Shape

Regular shapes are, well, consistent. Triangles, circles, and rectangles are basically immutable. The proportions can change, yet a triangle always has three-sides. Regular forms can be dissected into smaller regular shapes. When the pieces are reconstituted, the new shapes' total area is equal to the original one.

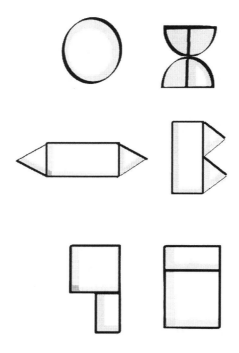

Math lesson aside, people are a bit like regular shapes. They are made of parts that are similar across the whole species. But, when you get down to it, there are infinite ways that people are different. At an emotional and psychic level, we are changeable. However, like in the conservation of area in the shapes, how we employ the parts of the whole is up to you. Said simply, feel free to grow and change. You won't lose anything that you need.

Shaping Self

Regular shapes can be combined in numerous ways. Much of the built environment around us is predicated on this fact.

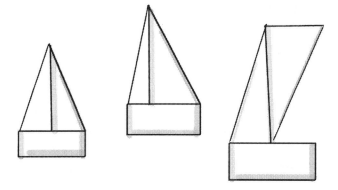

Your average weekday is split between work and personal time. This book asks you to think of each of those building blocks separately, but always keep in mind that they are interrelated.

The first feat of imagination can start here. Imagine your childhood at the time you developed the foundation for adulthood, like the solid rectangular foundation. Once you started your career, you evolved just as your working-self grew. Both parts of your life are pictured here as triangles.

For some people, their work fuels their growing persona. Their work triangle is broader than their personal life one. For others, work barely transformed their self at all. Their work triangle is thin and narrow.

One's relationship between the work and personal life can change over time. Starting out, your work-life may consume your time and encompass your personality. As time goes on, your personal life may come into balance or take over. This particular interrelationship between work and personal could be represented by the triangle positioned with the base upward.

Machine Learning

This model offers one visualization of the relationship between work and a person, with the "work" side of the machine being much more robust than the "you" side.

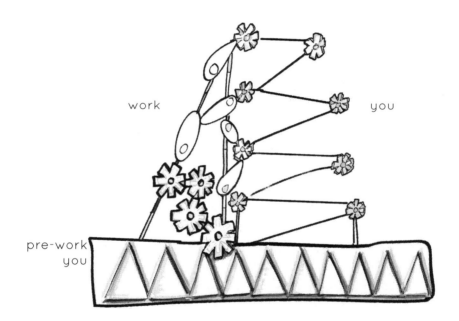

Draw your work-life balance machine. Show the relationship between these two parts of your life today as a crazy,
imaginary machine. Don't think too hard. And, don't judge
yourself. Just draw what comes to your mind.

You

Step 1: Purge Negativity

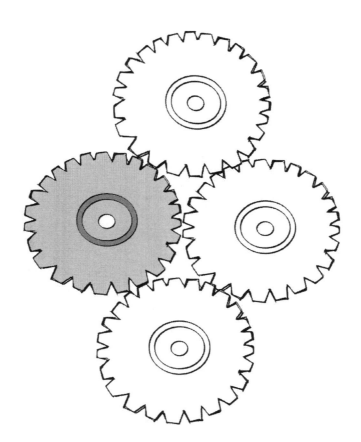

Purging negativity is best experienced as a slow controlled release. Don't do too many exercises at once. Once you finish a task, turn the page and don't look back right away. While you are focused on getting out your negativity, you might find that you will feel bummed. If so, do more basic self-care tasks. Also, try not to let your negativity spill into your interpersonal relationships.

Jade

The highest echelons of ancient Chinese society used jade suits to protect bodies for the afterlife. It's a useful visual metaphor when you think of being jaded. Metaphorically, we cover ourselves in assumptions, sarcasm, and negative expectations to protect ourselves from disappointment.

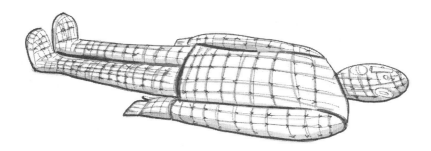

No one gets to adulthood without being a little jaded. Now, being a little jaded is okay. You need to keep yourself protected. But, a full shield prevents you from letting anything in. The key is understanding when your reticence is helpful.

Focus on understanding when your ideas are based in empirical information. For example, you might think "People hate going out in the snow so we shouldn't run an expensive program in the winter." You are working from experience there. In other words, try to disentangle cynicism and experience.

Another metaphor might be the comma-shaped jade ornaments that were found in tombs of ancient, influential Koreans. Scholars believe these jewels may have been symbols of wealth and power.

Let's use these metaphors to help us.
- Brainstorm all the things about which you are jaded.
- Imagine yourself divesting of these ideas.
- Pick a few ideas that you want to keep.
- Review these topics. Which ones are driven by experience?
- Keep the useful experiences. Write these alongside the jade jewels.
- Use the subsequent spread for this activity.

Jade, pt. 2

Recap: Keep this metaphor in mind.

Write the jaded thoughts that you want to give up.

The few critical judgments that you maintain:

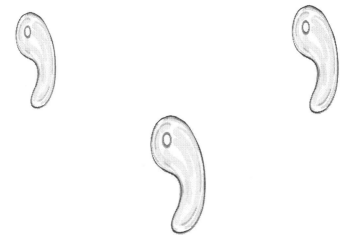

Anger

Robots continue to improve. Soon, robots will be able to act in ways that mimic people, like using emotion as a decision-making impetus. But, currently, if a robot pops a gasket, it will be a malfunction rather than a pique of anger.

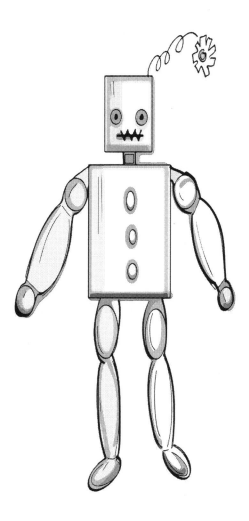

Anger is a highly individualized and situational emotion. A person might explode EVERY time they are angry. Another might only blow when their mother makes them mad and avoid all other angering situations. While some angry reactions can be useful, most are detrimental.

- Spend some time thinking of the last three times you were angry. Describe the situation.
- Then try to diagnose yourself: explosive, passive-aggressive, avoidance, sarcasm.
- Try to find a pattern.
- Create some if-then statements to generalize about your anger.
- Now, that you have a better sense of your anger rhythm, you can see places to short-circuit this cycle. Like, you always explode when your mom calls you at work, so you text your mom pro-actively during the day.

1

Anger, pt. 2

To recap: Spend some time thinking of the last three times you were angry.

- Describe the situation.
- Then try to diagnose yourself: explosive, passive-aggressive, avoidance, sarcasm.
- Try to find a pattern.
- Create some if-then statements to generalize about your anger.
- Look for places to short-circuit this cycle.

2

3

Annoyance

Think of when you have a tiny pebble in your shoe or a bit of something in your teeth. That small thing grows in importance, and you can't concentrate on anything else. Once you remove that irritation, you can go about your business.

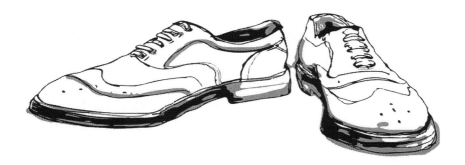

Make a list of those small irritations in life that drive you nuts. Be exhaustive. Be truthful. Add to this list as they come up.

Now, try to think of ways you can remove them. For some, it might mean changing your behavior. Others might require sharing your issue with friends and family. For many, however, you will just need to find a way to ignore or avoid these annoyances for the sake of sanity.

Other people

Even the most generous person doesn't get along with everyone. You can have genuine reasons to dislike people. But, then other people just rub you the wrong way.

- Catalog all the people who rub you the wrong way. Be brutal with your feelings. Be okay with going way back in time. Create a list of at least 12 people.
- Now, what rubs you the wrong way? Is it a big issue or a small one? Is it ideological? Or is it interpersonal?
- Finally, review the list of issues. How many of them fall into the category of ideological? Often, these will be issues that you can't overlook.
- How many are interpersonal?
- This activity continues on the next spread.

Other people, pt. 2

Your list continued:

- Finally, review the list of issues. Copy down your inter-personal issues here.
- For the interpersonal issues, how many are problems that you share? Reflect on these characteristics that annoy you.

Share Share

Many collection objects, when poised inert on their podiums, only evoke their original use. Functional objects, like this megaphone, go from loud things to quiet monuments of a time. Imagination becomes a bridge between passive to active.

At this point, you have been able to share some specific negative feelings. But, there might still be more within you.

- Pretend you have this megaphone in hand.
- What issues would you scream? What makes you nuts? Bonkers? Spitting angry? Write them down.
- Once you are done, take stock. How many of these are things that you actually tell other people? How many are things that you don't talk about? How many are issues that you can change? What is out of your control?

Metaphorically sharing this way, to yourself, can feel like a release. Do this periodically if you feel like you will burst with negatively. (You can also actually yell your issues. But, for some people, screaming is not cathartic and is scary.)

Still-Life

The Dutch were well-known for their love of still-life paint-
ings, chocked full of the best of what 17th-century life
had to offer. Some of these works had a double meaning.
Half-eaten fruit and clocks would remind the viewer that
life was fleeting.

Holding onto excessive negativity is a way of focusing on the half-empty nature of existence. While the temporary quality of life can feel overwhelming, you can also focus on the half-full glass.

This exercise invites you to turn a negative feeling into a positive one.

- Find *one* negative idea or habit you hope to improve.
- Decide for this week that you will do one small positive thing to counteract that habit. You could take a deep breath or touch your toes when you do that negative thing.
- Do this practice for seven days.
- Tally the times you do it each day. Take notes about the situation in which these negative habits occur.
- After the week, reflect on your notes. Look for patterns. You might find you are more likely to act in this negative manner when you are hungry or that drive-time is your witching hour. You might see that you do this negative thing less over the week.
- Keep up with this practice until you get out of the habit of your negative act.

Step 2: Focus on the Positive

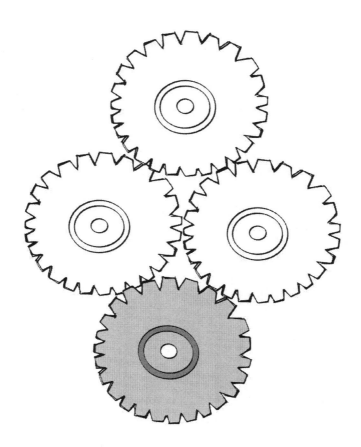

In this section, we will go through a series of activities to help you focus on the positive aspects of yourself. In addition to going through these practices, make sure to indulge in exercise, good food, and plenty of sunshine. Go out of your way to be kind to yourself.

Line

Lines are an essential element of art. Thick, thin, windy, straight, they come in many forms. Young children are good at filling pages with lines of every variety and texture.

This exercise is a good way to get yourself ready to move from negative to positive:

- Continue the line on the facing page. As you do, let your mind wonder and then bring your focus back to the line.
- Turn back to this spread periodically. Eventually, you will be able to meditate on this line for longer amounts of time. You will also completely cover these pages.

Period Rooms

Some objects and viewers benefit being installed in a manner that evokes the original context. Living history museums go one better. They allow visitors to immerse themselves in historic spaces, like stepping back to colonial America or standing on the floor of an industrial manufacturing shop. These installations help you fuse your present to the object's past.

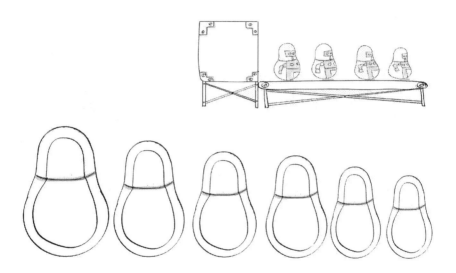

When you look back at a picture of yourself in kindergarten, you might have a sense of dislocation. You remember feeling pretty grown up. But, the person in the photograph is but a little kid. There is likely a kernel of truth both in your memory and the document of that moment.

As you mature, all of those phases in your life exist within you, like a set of nesting dolls. Those elements of yourself are within you but sometimes obscured by a subsequent stage.

This exercise invites you to excavate the best of your:
- Try to think back to 5 critical periods in your life. Choose ones that feel like important transitional moments.
- Spend time remembering decisive situations from that time. Negative thoughts will come into your mind. Allow them to, but try to focus on the positive ones.
- After remembering each period, write a one-sentence summary about what you liked about yourself from that time.
- Now, all of this is in you. If you don't feel like you have some of those characteristics now, try to focus on augmenting those parts of yourself.
- Use the subsequent spread for this activity.

Period Rooms, pt. 2

To recap: For each of your 5 critical moments, create a one-sentence summary about what you liked about yourself from that time.

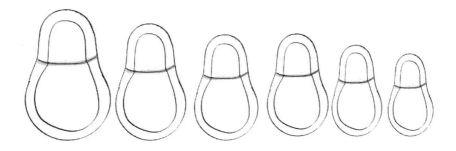

Common Life

Artifacts of daily life can illustrate the commonalities of human life. A cup has basically been cup-shaped since time immemorial. Bottle, jugs, and other containers for liquid are easy to pick out. They have a small opening to make pouring easy and evaporation hard.

Some things are so common that you don't spend enough time taking note of them. You probably have some habits that are so normal that you don't even notice them like you brush your teeth with your non-dominant hand.

This exercise will help you focus on the common positive elements in your life.
- Over the next few days, try to note every time you feel calm and/ or comfortable. Notice where you are and what you are doing. Be specific. Like, I am seated at my desk with hot coffee in the gray mug.
- Try to replicate that experience. Do you still feel like that?
- Modify the behavior slightly, and check your feeling. Like, try sitting at your desk with hot coffee in a black mug.
- Finally, from your list, try to extrapolate what common acts have been helping support positivity in your life.

Stars

Cut an apple horizontally to find a five-pointed star in the core. Flower petals often come in sets of five. You might be reading this while holding a pencil in your five fingers. Of course, starfish are five-sided. The pervasiveness of five-sided items in nature might relate to carbon-bonding angles and/or the Fibonacci sequence. Causes aside, once you learn a little fact like this, it is hard not to notice "fives" in nature.

What makes you a star? Keep a running list of the good in yourself. Get at least five, but try to get to fifteen or twenty-five.

Preserve and Display

Early museums were most definitely about things. These spaces were often installations of diverse objects, both natural and human-made, often safely displayed under glass.

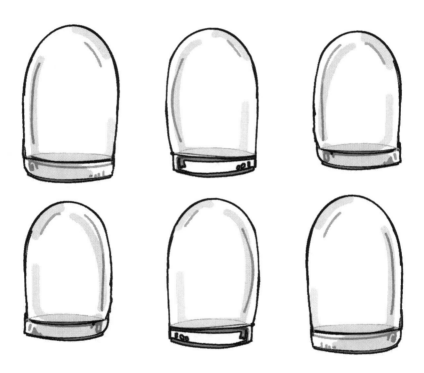

People display valuables under glass so that they can be shown safely. In other words, they want people to see this item but want no harm come to this treasure.

This activity helps you develop a display of your most prized personal characteristics:

- Think about yourself. Brainstorm traits that you value but fear sharing.
- Write each of these characteristics in the cloches on the facing page. You can write them in neat handwriting. Or, you can draw symbols that will remind you of these characteristics. Either way, just make sure that looking at them feels good.
- Now consider ways that you could expose these strengths safely. Let's say you value your sense of humor, but are too shy to make jokes in front of people. Try to make jokes on a closed FB page where you are already comfortable.

A Shield

Shields kept you safe in warfare. But, in times of peace, armor and shields became luxury-ware. Fine gentlemen might have personal elements added to these beautiful metal objects, like their coat of arms or family motto. After all, this excellent armor would never be sullied in war, and the motto would be seen easily.

Family mottoes are passed down through generations. Imagine yourself free from the bonds of history.

Develop your own motto.
- Start by reviewing the section.
- Write the big ideas that you have learned about yourself.
- Add any other things you might feel are missing.
- Set this exercise aside. Reflect. Try thinking about it when you are driving or showering. What ideas still stick with you?
- Now, get literary. Craft the most significant idea into a short phrase, say five words or less.
- Use your most exceptional handwriting to put down your final motto here. Make it beautiful.

Step 3: Imagine

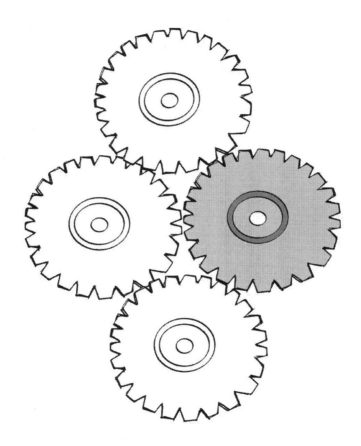

While you have used imagination for the activities up to this point, now that creative skill becomes the focus of your work. Try to suspend disbelief and embrace your creative side.

Sprint

The animal world's fastest runner, the Cheetah is 6-foot one inches long. The unsuspecting prey might not be aware that this big cat is in hot pursuit. At speeds of up to 75 miles per hour, this predator's spots blur, making the ideal camouflage.

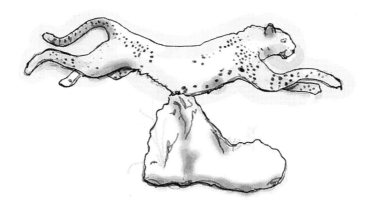

A colleague once told me this fact when explaining she is as tall as the big cat is long. This tall, red-headed woman, who was 75 years old if she was a day, proceeded to share how she liked to imagine moving like a cheetah.

Imagination might take some practice. And, even if you are an expert daydreamer, imagination sprints help you work on positivity in your creativity. Spend at least 5 minutes daily with these.

Here are a few prompts to get you started. Add more as they come to you. Imagine being:
- In your ideal work role
- At a pivotal moment in the past
- On the moon
- Underwater
- Walking on the ceiling
- Working at a dream job
- Working on your worst job imaginable
- On a desert island
- A character in a favorite novel
- In the original context of your favorite museum object

Sprint, pt. 2

More space for your sprint notes.

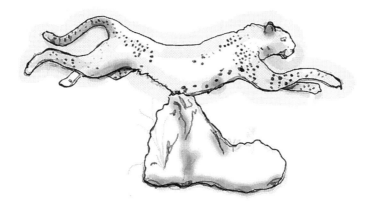

Precious Bottles

Luxury goods, like perfume, were often packaged in equally precious bottles. Your senses would be engaged in putting on this toiletry. Your eyes would be dazzled by the opalescent glass, and your touch would enjoy the smoothness of the bottle. Finally, your nose would be engaged by the perfume.

Senses are one of the most evocative elements in memory. A whiff of pine might take you to holidays past. The smell of markers might remind you of preschool days.

Develop an ideal sense memory chart for yourself.
- Begin by brainstorming sense memories that bring you joy. Spend time with this step.
- Imagine a situation where you might find a number of these sensory conditions. (If are sensitive to sensory stimuli, just choose one sense memory to focus on.)
- Now, fill in the chart with the sense memories that match the emotions.
- Use these sense memories when you need to evoke that specific feeling.

Relaxed   *Confident*   *Energized*   *Calm*

Thoughtful   *Happy*   *Content*   *Excited*

Capital Idea

Religious spaces often functioned as visual academies instructing believers in the tenants of the faith. In medieval Christian churches in Europe, teachable moments would be carved in stone, poised above church-goers atop columns. These historiated capitals showed a choice snippet that would evoke a well-known story for the adherent.

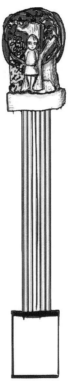

We are all the heroes of our lives if you tell the story right.

- Find some moments when you were the hero, or where you embodied your most valued characteristics.
- Pick one to sketch as a capital.
- Before you sketch, try to think of the moment you will capture. This moment should symbolize why you feel this was a heroic story. Write why this felt heroic. Think of ways that you could encapsulate those feelings in visuals.
- Sketch your capital here. Make yourself the hero you are.

Poster Child

In the mid-20th century, Hollywood studios used artists to create bold movie posters that showcased the stars. The movie *glitterati* were shown as larger than life—a glamorous persona rather than a real person.

Today, designers often use "personas" to plan projects. In this case, a persona is like the old Hollywood definition in that they are simplified sketches of people.

In developing a project, you create a handful of sample narratives based on your research of your audience. So, rather than planning for "visitors", you can plan for Persona: Joe, the middle-aged man who likes to garden and watch war movies. Your ideas are better when you have a specific target in mind.

In this exercise, you turn personas on their head. We will be using the persona, short verbal sketches of people, but to describe different aspects of yourself.

- Use your notes up to this point to create three to five distinct personas that represent aspects of yourself.
- Begin by flipping back through the book. What different aspects of yourself aspects can you discern?
- Next start writing. For each persona, start with a descriptive title. For example, "Persona: Runner-Girl."
- Write two short sentences that describe each persona's motivations. Like, "Runner-Girl likes to get out and move her body. She would rather run than read."
- Add a graphic, like an emoji, to help you remember each persona.
- You will now use these elements to help you with your future imagining and planning.
- Use the subsequent spread for your work.

Poster Child, pt. 2

Use this spread for your final personas.

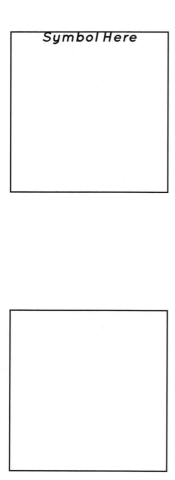

Symbol Here

Type

Typewriters are collection objects that connect you to the recent past. The function of the typewriter remains. Most people use a keyboard, to some degree, on their phone or computer. The sensation of using a typewriter, however, is divided by generation. Many people alive used a typewriter when other options didn't exist.

But, even if you never used one, imagine drafting a note with this typewriter. Hear the clickety-clack of the keys. Feeling the gentle resistance as you type out a word. Imagine the sound of the carriage sliding back into place.

- Turn back to your personas. Try to use these to help you imagine possible future experiences you will have.
- Write a 6-word story that foretells a possible positive future for each persona, for example, "Finishing the marathon, Runner-Girl feels victorious."
- Along with each story, draw an evocative object, like runner girl's smelly shoes and the persona symbol.
- Make sure to focus on the future throughout this exercise. The objects can be items you currently own, however, though they need to be associated with the future. For example, they can be your current running shoes, but the story needs to be about the future experience with these shoes.

The Museum of You

Now you have many possible futures from your personas. Take those with the best of your ideas in the positivity section to develop a collection of items that represent your ideal future self.

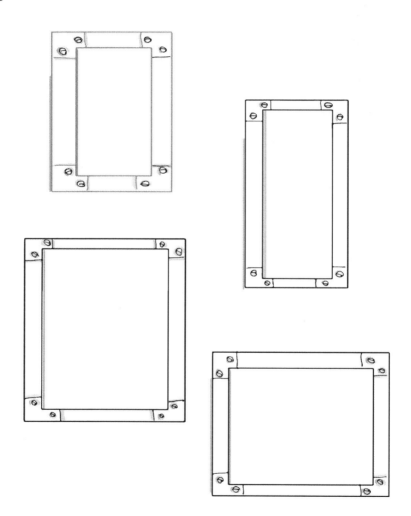

Use both pages. The items can be real or imaginary. Start by adding to these frames.

Step 4: Plan

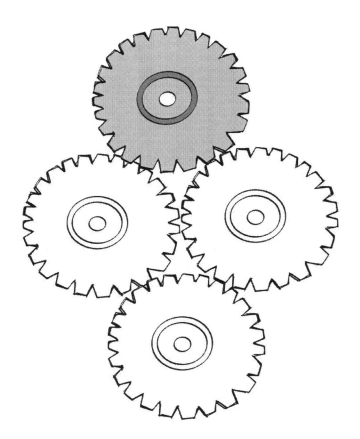

In this section, you focus on making broad plans to maintain the best you.

Weaving

All spiders make silk. This evolutionary advantage
helped arachnids to catch prey, protect their eggs, and
build inhabitable structures. The spider weaves threads
into an interconnected, durable, flexible web.

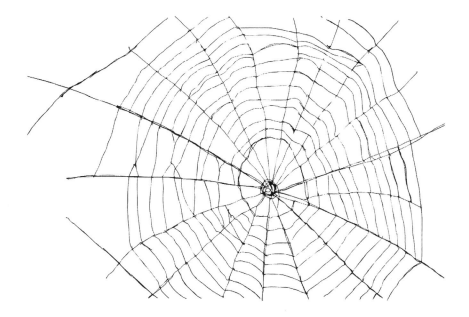

Develop a web that draws out the ideal you.

- Start by writing your name in the middle. Next, add the big ideas and goals that you have distilled throughout part 1. Draw lines between those ideas and your name.
- Then start breaking down those ideas. What do you need to do to achieve those goals? Write those. Draw lines to connect them to related concepts.
- Keep going. Don't worry if this is messy. You are the only one who will see this.

Cutting it

Some human endeavors attest to our fortitude. The pyramids, the moon landing, and the invention of flight all come to mind. But, even apparently banal tools evoke the strength of their owners. Many collections hold ancient implements, like stone blades. Imagine being that person who carefully fashioned a rock into a blade. The creation of simple tools is one of those activities that bring near instant rewards. As soon as a sharp edge is achieved, you can get to spearing dinner.

The spear craftsman had a clear mission that he achieved, as evidenced by the existence of the blade. If he wrote a mission statement, it might be: "Make tools that kill." His vision statement might have been, "Expand tool-making forever."

The first step in planning is to develop your mission and vision statements. A mission statement articulates your aims. Your vision statement, on the other hand, is where you aspire towards a future you. Each should be only one-two sentences in clear, succinct language. You want phrases that you could recite without taxing your memory.

Spend time reviewing your notes. Your "positive" section should help point you in the direction of your mission. Your "imagine" section should support your work on the vision.

Use this space for your final statements. Use extra paper for your notes.

Navigating

The astrolabe was a highly prized tool for sea-faring explorers. With this device, you no longer had to fear being completely lost at the open sea. A skilled navigator needs just this tool, the stars above, and his know-how to plan the ship's course.

A strategic plan is a path between your mission statement and your vision statement. Like the astrolabe, it is a navigation aid, rather than a set of a directional statements.

- Start by looking at your mind map. Can you make connections between topics? Are there trends in your goals or planned actions?
- Try to come up with 3-4 sentences that summarize your path from now to your planned future.
- Each statement should be flexible but offer direction. For example, if your goal is to work at an executive level, you might come up with the following statement: Achieve the education or experience necessary to apply for a promotion.

Pipeline

Pipes were a significant jump in human civilization. Liquids, both clean and not, could be moved using gravity without direct human effort. Pipes were a considerable jump for the civilized living. With gravity, liquids could be moved where people wanted. Pipes underlie all American cities. You don't even need to think about them as you reach for the tap. The water will still come out.

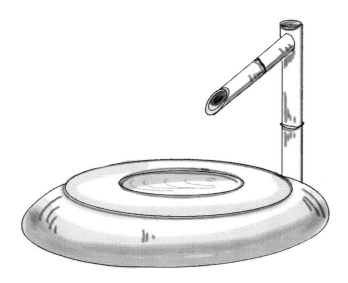

Kanban is a method that comes from software development. Basically it is a flexible tool to help you visualize a moving process.

- Take one part of your strategic plan.
- Write the subsidiary tasks to make it happen on post-it notes. Be granular.
- Copy the Kanban chart onto a large board or poster.
- Physically move the post-it notes down the pipeline as you finish them. Being granular should mean that you have lots of smaller tasks that you can move down the pipeline quickly.
- As you achieve an element, then move the note. Moving that post-it feels so good, I promise.

To Do	Doing	Done

Signs

Signs were a significant way to communicate ideas to a group of people long before neon. The best sign says a volumes but simply.

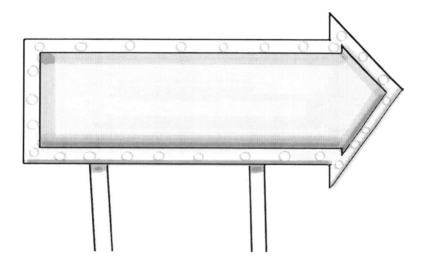

Success usually requires two things: a carrot and a stick. Develop a system of signifiers to help you with each inducement.

First, create a positive feedback loop. Think of a way that you can treat yourself when you accomplish part of your plan. Make it something simple, so that you can treat yourself when you finish even the smallest part of your project.

Second, surround yourself with positive messages. These could literally be signs. But, you could also just beautify the corner of your room where you work in this book. In other words, make your physical space help support your changing mental space.

You
&
Work

Step 1: Purge the Negativity about Work

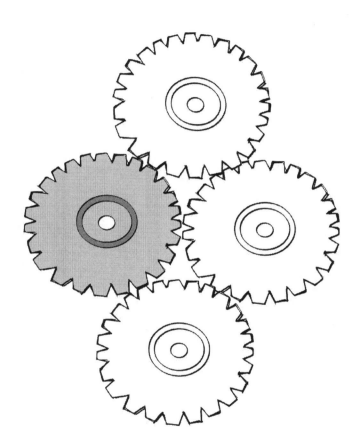

While you have already purged negativity about yourself, you need to spend time on work-related bad feelings. As with the previous section, try not to share your negativity with others.

Junk

Good design fuses form and function pleasingly. Often trash cans that make it into museum collections score high points for style. The functional receptacles in museums can be there thanks to their provenance. Few, if any, trash cans are in museums due to the junk they housed.

Garbage cans are spaces where trash lives until it is completely removed from your office. Metaphorically, however, you might be filling yourself with junk. You might be filling yourself with bad feelings about work. Use this spread to unload negative opinions and stories about your job. Keep going until you feel like you have taken out the trash. When you are honestly done, rip out these sheets. Ball them up and throw them out.

Fakes

A good fake is one that seems real. All forgeries are fake, but the reverse is not always true. A forgery is a fake meant to fool others.

Some people are just straight up false. They put on an act. Sometimes they are putting on an act for everyone, including themselves. You know these people. They are not comfortable in their skin. They are also often their own worst enemies.

Some people treat you nicely when they want something and then turn away to speak poorly about you. These people are human forgeries. Being around people like this can feel draining. Their political machinations can have a detrimental effect on the workplace.

Use this space to unmask the forgeries in your world. Write about them. When you finish, deface this page with beautiful graffiti. As to the fakes, let them be.

Under Glass

Fluid preservation began in the 17th century. This method allowed scientists to fix specimens so they won't deteriorate. These creatures can, then, remain on the shelf for careful examination—a challenging feat when a live sample is fleeing for its life.

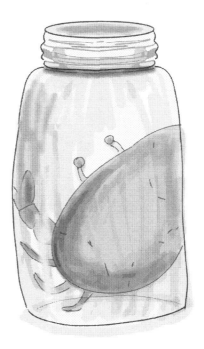

Phrases like fax machines, spreadsheets, duplexing with stapling might give you unhappy flashbacks. Much of work is learned on the ground, sometimes with time-spent and tears. People skills can be even more hard won. Humans rarely come with directions.

This exercise is in the negative section because you might have some residual bad feelings associated with some work skills. The goal is to maintain the memory of the ability while exorcising the negative emotions.

- Brainstorm some of the parts of work that you hate. Try to parse out those experiences. Is this hatred due to the skills or an interpersonal relationship? If it is about the skills, circle them.
- Now, look at your collection of skills. Write out a sentence that encompasses your bad feelings. For example, you might remember that you had to fight with the fax machine, all the while being judged by the creepy assistant.
- Finally, write the skills on the jars on the next spread. You want to hold onto the skill but let go of the bad feelings. The skill helps you; the bad feelings don't.

Under Glass, pt. 2

Recap: Write your best skills on the jars. You want to hold onto the skill but let go of the bad feelings. The skill helps you; the bad feelings don't.

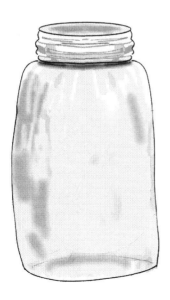

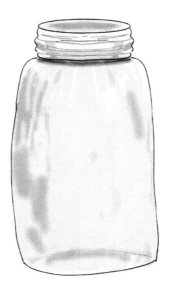

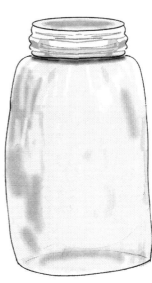

Here Be Monsters

The basilisk could kill you with a glance. This fierce, hopefully mythical, creature might have become part of popular imagination thanks to travelers' tales of cobras. While hooded snakes are terrifying in their own right, the human imagination added supernatural powers to a natural predator.

In some projects, a colleague can take on nearly super-human powers. You imagine they are focused on making you feel miserable. These issues are a combination of their actions and your reactions. But, that doesn't make your feelings any less critical. In your mind, they feel more like a basilisk then a garden-variety cobra.

This exercise uses humor to demystify your work monsters. Spend some time imagining slaying your work monsters.
- Start by writing their name.
- Draw a caricature of this person.
- Write what makes you feel like they are a monster, include their actions and your reactions.
- Draw in the tool you will use to slay them. Go for funny, like being attacked by squid and cacti, not gory.
- Use the subsequent spread for your attacks.

Here Be Monsters

Slay work monsters here.

Contraption

Science museums' "collections" are often ideas. In installations, visitors add their input and, in return, earn a reward.
This type of active engagement makes the learning stick.

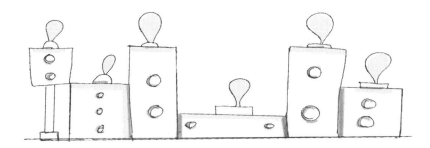

Negativity is a challenging human emotion. You can find yourself in a terrible rut, where all you are doing is complaining. We have all been there. Diversion can be one way to break the cycle. Imagination is another.

This exercise invites you to imagine that you are trying to use your complaints to fuel the Constructive Compliant Contraption.
- Fill this page with your complaints.
- As you write a claim, make the balloons on the device slightly bigger.
- Then take a deep breath.
- Keep going until the balloons reach the top of the page. Then you are done. Imagine the balloons exploding. What does it sound like?
- Take five deep breaths.
- After this, every time you start complaining, take a deep breath and imagine the balloon machine.

Failure

The Wright Brothers got their manned airplane off the ground in 1903. Before them, scores of inventors tried and tried again to achieve the then-unprecedented feat of giving humans the ability to fly. The Wright Brothers themselves created many prototypes before their 1903 plane. They saw these early models as research, not failures.

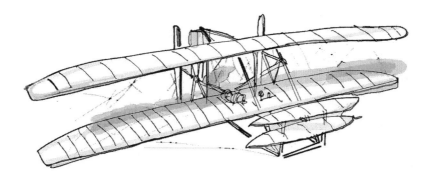

Failure is a word with a certain weight. It seems to be embody the heavy emotions of loss, embarrassment, sadness, shame, shock, and disappointment. Failure feels bad. Failure has finality. Instead, if you think of that moment as a misstep, or even as moment of recalibration, you can turn the failure into something positive.

Write out your biggest failure. Be exhaustive in your storytelling. Include your feelings and your perceptions of the feelings of others. Afterward, turn to the next spread.

Failure, pt. 2

Focus on the emotions associated with your story. Reflect on your perceptions of other people's emotions. How many of those feelings might be projecting your own ideas of success on them? How many are truthful? What evidence did you have for their opinions?

Now, look at that story, as if it wasn't you. What opportunities do you see for this person? What tips might you offer this person to learn from this failure?

Calculating

An abacus is an ideal calculation tool on the fly. With a little practice, you can make complex calculations fast. Abacuses in museums collections are usually special ones like exemplars of the type either in their manufacture or provenance.

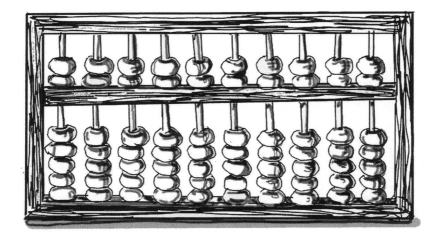

Museums have their own culture. The label for the abacus, while made for this book, epitomizes some of our museum existence, namely prizing exemplary objects. The need for collection excellence has ramifications for the work-force, certainly. And, this is just one issue that one feels working in this field.

As part of that culture, you are uniquely capable of de-termining the pros and cons of working in this culture. Be thoughtful and exhaustive. Take a break to reflect. Come back to finish your list. Feel free to use extra paper.

Pros

Cons

Step 2: Foster Positivity at Work

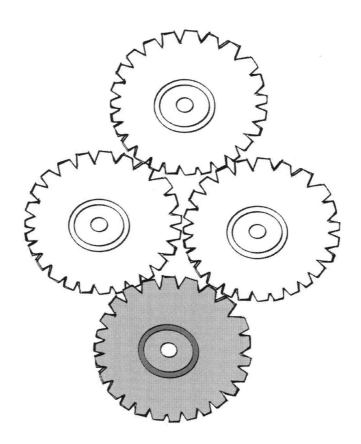

This part might be one of the most challenging parts of the whole book. Some books blithely suggest that you find the good in everything, which is not realistic. No matter how optimistic you hope to be, outside factors will try to break your vibe. You will learn to look for the positive in situations. In other words, you will learn to see the glass as half-full when the cup is 1/2 full. You won't learn to pretend the glass is half-full when it is empty.

Object Lessons

Let's turn the tables a bit. Spend some time doing your own object lessons. Find a collection object in any institution to draw 10 times. Focus on the object, not the sketch. If your mind wanders, refocus by concentrating on the lines you are drawing.

Why do you work at a museum?

No lead in on this one. Just that question. Write all the good reasons that you work in a museum or collection-based/ knowledge-work institution.

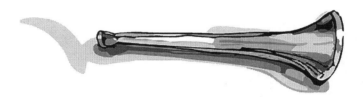

Light

Small ceramic lanterns transformed people's daily life. Their working time was no longer constrained by sunlight. You could move your lantern where you needed extra illumination to get your work done.

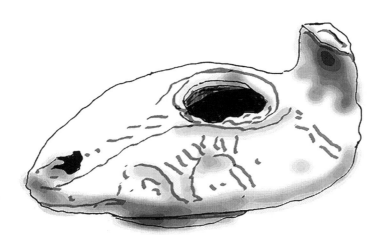

Spend some time with this metaphor. Where do you feel like you need a little more positivity to get your work done? Try to think about experiences that should be easier than they are. Then brainstorm ways you can re-frame them to decrease the challenges.

In Stone

History includes some crucial documents preserved in stone for posterity, like the Code of Hammurabi and Moses' now-lost Ten Commandments tablets. Stone has the advantage of lasting for ages. However, one doesn't go through the trouble of taking a hammer and chisel to a hard rock for a draft idea. You set into stone thoughts that are worthy.

Can you come up with ten steadfast truths about your work self that you won't break? These ideas can be significant, like your philosophy on work friendship, or frivolous like your sartorial standards. Ideally, you want a mix of profound insights and humorous ones. Once you finalize them, write them here in permanent ink. If all else goes crazy at work, you will have these truths.

Weight

Vast fortunes, from the gold of West Africa to the silk of China, went through the hands of the global chain of traders. Traders became wealthy by being systematic. They carefully measured and double-measured their wares. Each trader worth their store kept a full set of weights, ones that they trusted.

Spend time thinking about your greatest professional strengths. Start with measurable powers, like you are an able typist. Once you have cataloged these, move onto intangible abilities, like interpersonal skills. These strengths have served you well, but writing them out will add weight to them.

Armor

Renaissance European princes often owned parade armor for use on official and ceremonial occasions. These finely wrought metalwork masterpieces were emblazoned with symbols like mythical animals. These luxury wearables glorified the prowess of the wearer.

In the first section, you created a shield with your personal motto. Now, create your matching suit of parade armor. Review your notes on your strengths at work. Come up with an animals or mythological figures that represent these powers. Fill this armor with symbols of the things that make you good at work.

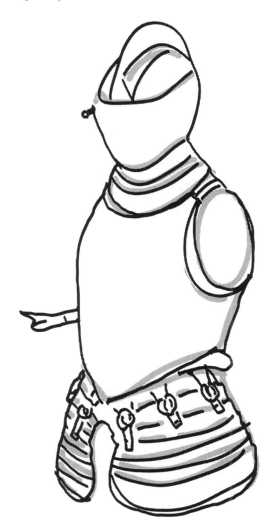

Odes

Odysseus did not mean to get stuck on this island. He certainly didn't mean to chug that wine. And, he isn't quite sure how he kept falling into bed with that nice girl, Calypso. But, he didn't want to be a rude guest.

Isn't this how the Odyssey goes?

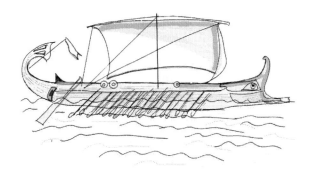

The poets of old created verse in honor of heroic exploits and less than noble love affairs.

Commemorate one of your incredible work adventures in verse. Feel free to be humorous.

Scale

In a scale, weights are placed in the tray opposite items of unknown weight until both sides are balanced, or of equal heft. In common parlance, a scale can be used to describe a set of colors to help you make sure your photograph is not off-color. You can play a scale on the piano, a standard set of notes. Scales are standards against which other things are measured.

In the last exercise in this section, you will develop your values. These professional values will be used to help you weigh your future plans. You have already figured out your truths and your strengths. So, you are nearly there. This section is a number of spreads, but try to go slowly over the section.

Let's think about where you are today. Look at your work environment. Find five objects that you use regularly. Sketch them. Annotate them with notes about color, wear, and imperfections. In other words, document them thoroughly. Finally, write what you value about these objects. You might need to think a little. At first, it might be hard to think of the value of a stapler, say. But, if you use it every day, then it must have value. Next you will explore your ideas about these objects.

Scale, pt. 2

What do your five objects say about what you value at work? You might see a trend towards efficiency. You might be interested in communication and community, and so appreciate your conference room table. Start by writing those values under the word "now."

Afterward, develop a timeline of your work history. What were the most important things in your office at your first job? Why? Choose one or two positions in-between then and now to fill out your work history.

Now

_____

Reflect on your work timeline. Star times that you were most proud and/or happy. Circle values that overlap more than one position.

Now you have a direction to create your value statements.

First Job

Scale, pt. 3

Over the process of the exercises in this book, you have investigated yourself. Look back. Take notes here. Look for critical themes about what makes you happy or value.

Finally, answer these questions:
Of which work achievement are you most proud? Of which achievement have you received the most positive feedback? What aspects of work make you feel most satisfied?

Scale, pt. 4

Now put all the parts of this activity together.

Find five things about your work self that you value based on the notes from this activity. Catalog them. Dissect your ideas. Extrapolate your values.

Here is a short list of values to help you start your work: Empathy, Diligence, Discipline. Discretion, Compassion, Boldness, Calmness, Integrity, Creativity, Honesty, Curiosity, and Respect. You will want to brainstorm more.

Then, craft short sentences that encompass your particular value. Each phrase should be short and succinct. For example: Exemplify Integrity.

Step 3: Imagine

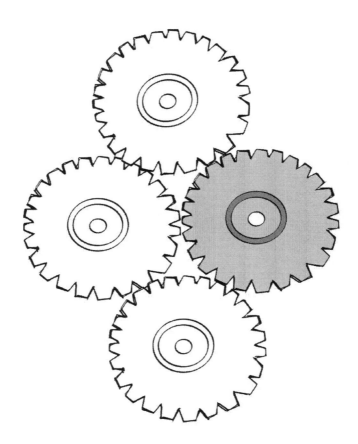

This section builds on skills you already have. Who hasn't daydreamed about a possible outcome at work?

Missives

Letters are incredibly personal artifacts. They were meant for but two people: the sender and the intended. The contents are then folded up, enclosed, and then passed on. They are like secrets passed in plain sight.

Working life is a bit like group projects in high school. You usually have a couple of people doing it well, and the others are, well, not. Being able to navigate groups and do collective work is a learned skill. Think back to the people who helped you hone your team-work skills. They might have directly helped you. Or they might have modeled the type of behavior that results in success. Imagine you are writing them thank you notes. What would you tell them?

Missives, pt. 2

Now, look back at your timeline. Who were the people who helped you when you were at the happiest times in your career? Drop them an imaginary line. Be specific in your appreciation. What exactly did they do to help you become the person you are now?

Chat

Writing a label is easy. You distill a lifetime of research into 60 interesting, thoughtful, and evocative words. Basically, you spend 4 minutes per word, minimum, to create something that visitors read for 4 minutes total maximum. But, if one person is engaged, you have done your job. [48]

Can you write a label about your ideal work self?

- 60 words max.
- Make sure to lead with a strong sentence.
- Put in details that add to the reader's appreciation. Exclude anything that requires more than 60 words to explain.
- Use words that don't need a dictionary for the general population.
- Write to be understood.

Light It Up

By the 1870s, electric lights were commercially viable in the United States. This momentous change for civil society was not an overnight innovation. In the prior decades, inventors experimented with various forms of bulbs. The now ubiquitous light bulb is a testament to human industry.

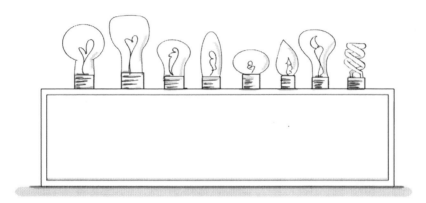

Imagine you have infinite money to spend on a passion project. Start by writing down your passion project goals. Then brainstorm all of the ways you could use the money. No wrong answer.

Ursa Major

If a bear must attack you, hope that it isn't a polar bear. Unlike the black bear, people do not easily survive a tussle with the cold-weather ursine.

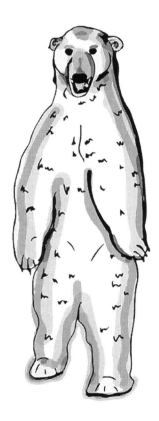

Most museum professionals will not find themselves in the path of a polar bear during work. But, what is the absolute worst case scenario that could happen at your job? Think adventure film. Write a short story about this terrible situation with yourself as the hero.

Sit-In

Designers Charles and Ray Eames worked on the cutting edge of technology. For example, they used innovative practices to create the bent plywood form. The resulting chair had a visually appealing sinuous shape that was also ideal for a comfortable respite.

The Eames chair didn't vary from the essence of the chair too greatly, but just enough to be ground-breaking. Imagine your job but better. Make tweaks that transform what you are doing into what you might enjoy doing. Write out your imagined job description.

Express Yourself

Japanese Noh Theater was a refined and much-beloved classical art form. Performers, historically, wore masks. Actors wore these highly stylized facial accoutrement and instead used their gestures to emote during scenes.

We have all been sitting in meetings where you can only make it through by putting up a blank facade. Imagine the worst meeting ever. Now, picture this meeting as if it were a performance, like a comic play, Noh performance, or musical. You are the hero. You change the drudgery into productivity with joy. Draw this scene.

Blueprint

You are near the end of the "Imagine" phase. We have tackled many parts of museum life. But we haven't addressed the most significant element—the museum.

Make your best imaginary museum. If you want, design your collection-based knowledge-work institution. (This activity goes over multiple spreads.)

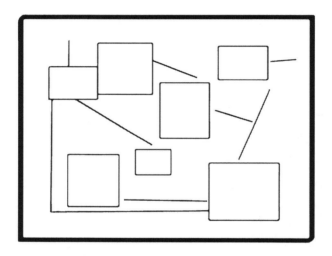

If you had infinite money, what would your imaginary museum be?

Name:

Mission:

Vision

Blueprint, pt. 2

Describe and draw your collection.

Keep going. What would it look like? Who would you serve? What would your visitors say?

Blueprint p.3

Write all your hopes for your imaginary museum across this spread. Use bright colors and lovely imagery.

Step 4: Plan

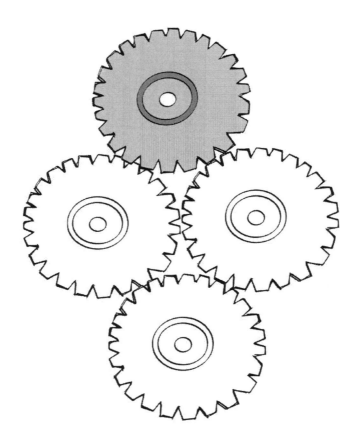

In the final section, you will find ways to weave the strands from previous sections into your plans.

Metaphor

At this point, you have seen X objects as metaphors for elements of life. Now I turn it over to you. For each activity in this section, you will be invited to do the exercise. Then, pick an object metaphor. These object metaphors are helpful because they become like a mnemonic. Think back on the activities in this book. Have you conflated some of the memories of the activities with memories of the object metaphor?

Use this page for a running list of object metaphors that come into your mind:

Plan

The plan section will deviate from the rest of the book. Think of it as a capstone. In the first few sections of this book, you have been focused on discovering and dreaming. Now you are going to design some concrete ways to make the dreams happen.

Let's start where we began. Answer these questions. Don't look back. Don't think too hard. Answer in words and pictures. (After you are done, go back to your original quiz. Has anything changed?)

What are your three biggest dreams?

Who are you?

What makes you tick?

What makes you freeze?

What exhausts you?

What ignites you?

What is your greatest sadness?

What brings you unspeakable joy?

What makes you slow down?

What is your greatest desire?

On Your Own

Focus on your life outside of work. Begin by noting all the differences between your original survey and this one. Then go through your notes on your values. Where do you see places in your answer that don't reflect your values? What broad goals for yourself can you develop to line up your values with your survey answers? Make these goals doable and specific. Rather than saying, "be happy," find a concrete way to become happier, like "Do X five times a week to become happier."

Draw and annotate your visual mnemonic/ metaphor for this activity.

Line Up

You are not in an ideal state when your hopes and reality don't align. So, let's see how you line up. Compare your imaginary museum with the museum where you work. If you don't work in one, pick one that you know well. Where are there similarities? Differences? (This activity goes over two spreads.)

Similarities

Differences

Line Up, pt. 2

For the differences, are there elements that you can change? So, if your museum is not inclusive, can you start by working with colleagues to start an inclusion committee. This is also the moment for the tough question--are there things you can do where you are to make it better? If not, go your plan about finding a new place to be. And, if that position if not in a museum, its okay.

Draw and annotate your visual mnemonic/ metaphor for this activity.

Map

From your Line Up activity, try to develop three to five concrete goals and action statements about your work self. Don't take on too much. If your whole organization is messed up, it is. But, you might be able to make your office less crazy. (This activity goes over multiple spreads.)

Goal

1

2

Statement

Map, pt. 2

Goal

3

4

5

Statement

Map, pt. 3

Now, take each of your action statements and map them out. What steps are you going to take when? Be concrete. Give yourself deadlines.

Now

_____

Then

Map, pt. 4

Maps take you somewhere. Where are you headed? And what reward will you get when you arrive?

Draw and annotate your visual mnemonic/ metaphor for this activity.

Map, pt. 5

Alright, you know where you are going. You know when. So, draw a treasure map. Make it fabulous. Make it something that you want to use. But, make sure it includes your actual path.

Conclusion

This is the where our paths diverge. We have gone through the process twice, once focusing on you and then again to consider your relationship to work. Through each activity, ideally, you found yourself more able to feel more objective in decision-making and planning.

This process can take you through many challenges. Let's say you have a project that is making you lose your mind. Go through the four gears. You can re-use exercises from the book. Or, you can make up your own. (Don't think you can? Redo some of the imagination exercises, and then reconsider if you can.)

But before you close this book, reflect on what you have learned. I could write more concluding materials. I could wax poetic about the flexibility of the mind, and the ways that imagination can transform your thinking. I could remind you that a healthy positive mental state can't easily be formed without releasing your negativity. But, those are my conclusions from going through these activities.

The truth is that in process-based books the author is working in collaboration with the reader/ user. So, the conclusion that matters most is yours. What have you gotten out of all these projects? Spend some time reflecting and write your conclusions.

Your conclusion

about yourself

about work

about the process

Index

Thank you

I start by thanking my family who allowed me the time to sketch, think, and imagine. Thanks to my parents who watched the girls as I sat home late evenings getting the layout right; to my girls who put up with mommy when she said, just one more minute; and to Joe who stayed up beside me late into the night. Thank you for your support.

Great thanks to some people also:
To my beloved friends in the old department. I cherish all the memories of our good times from our cut-out of Jake, the ever-present treats, the wigs, and mostly the friendship. I will always think of our time in our dungeon office as a type of art supply-fueled Camelot, and I love all of you.

To Joellen DeOreo, my first boss. She is a woman of grace and intelligence. When I became a manager, I often thought of how I didn't match up to her model. I think of her often when I manage to diffuse a situation without anger.

To Suse Anderson and Jeffrey Inscho for inviting me to speak on the American Alliance of Museum's MuseoPunks. This book had started as a pipe dream. I don't know if it would have come to fruition if I hadn't publicly shared the plan on your podcast. You are lovely for this field.

To Chad Weinard and Jennifer Poleon who egged me on one day over a glass of wine. I am glad you told me to do this. And, to so many far away and kindred museum friends. I love finding you at conferences and online. You are kind and supportive. There is no room to share each of your names because this is a field where friendship is easily given and rarely lost. I appreciate you, friends.

About the Author & Illustrator

Seema Rao was born and raised in Cleveland, Ohio where she continues to reside. She loves to draw, eat, and read. But, mostly, she enjoys hanging out with her husband, daughters, and insanely easy-going dog.

She spent nearly 20 years working in museums. Now she serves as a consultant to institutions worldwide.

Active on social media, you can find her at:

Blog: www.brilliantideastudio.com/blog
Twitter: @artlust
Instagram: @artplayspace